Thierry He[r]

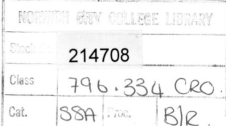

Andy Croft

Published in association with The Basic Skills Agency

Hodder Murray

A MEMBER OF THE HODDER HEADLINE GROUP

The Publishers would like to thank the following for permission to reproduce copyright material:

Photo credits
p.2 © Sipa Press/Rex Features; p.6 © Tony Marshall Copyright: Empics Sports Photo Agency; p.9 © Luca Bruno/AP Photo; p.14 © Rex Features; p.19 © Sporting Pictures UK Ltd/Rex Features; p.23 © Richard Young/Rex Features; p.25 © PA Photos/Empics.

Orders: please contact Bookpoint Ltd, 130 Milton Park, Abingdon, Oxon OX14 4SB. Telephone: (44) 01235 827720. Fax: (44) 01235 400454. Lines are open from 9.00–5.00, Monday to Saturday, with a 24-hour message answering service. Visit our website at www.hodderheadline.co.uk.

Cover photo © Carl de Souza/AFP/Getty Images
Typeset in 14pt Palatino by SX Composing DTP, Rayleigh, Essex.
Printed in Great Britain by CPI Bath.

A catalogue record for this title is available from the British Library

ISBN-10 0 340 90064 4
ISBN-13 978 0 340 90064 2

Contents

1 The Musketeer

He is fast.

He has quick feet and a great first touch.

He has fantastic ball control.

He has good balance and amazing vision.

He works hard.

His shooting is strong.

His finishing is deadly.

Thierry Henry is one of the most exciting strikers in the world.

Thierry Henry.

2 Beginnings

Thierry Daniel Henry was born
on 17 August 1977 in Paris, France.
His father Toni and his mother Maryse
came from the West Indies.

Thierry and his brother Willy
lived with their parents in a two-bedroom flat
in a tough part of Paris.
Thierry and his friends
played football on concrete.
They played against the walls
of the tower-blocks.
They dreamed of being famous footballers.
Thierry's favourite English team was Arsenal.

Thierry soon started playing
for local junior teams.
He was very fast.
(His uncle was the French 400-metre
hurdle champion.)
Thierry was very good.
When he was 13 he was playing
for an under-15 side.
One season he scored 77 goals
in 26 games for one team.

His mother wanted him to have a good education.
Thierry went to Alexander Fleming College
in Paris.

When he was 13 Thierry went for a trial
at the French National Football School.
Only 24 boys were chosen each year
to go to the school.
There were 800 boys there that day.
Thierry was chosen.

He was a pupil there for three years.
Among his friends were three boys
who would also play in the Premier League one day:
Louis Saha (Fulham and Manchester United),
William Gallas (Chelsea), and
Nicholas Anelka (Arsenal and Manchester City).
They became friends.
Saha used to stay with Thierry's family
in the holidays.

Thierry and Louis Saha.

3 France

When Thierry was 16 he joined Monaco.
The manager was called Arsène Wenger.
He knew that Thierry was special.
Wenger gave him his first game
when he was only 17.

In those days Thierry played as a winger
for Monaco.
But he still scored 32 goals in 119 games.
It is unusual for a winger to score so many goals.

Arsène Wenger then became manager of Arsenal.
In 1998 Arsenal tried to buy Thierry.
But Monaco said he was not for sale.

When Thierry was only 17
he played for France
in the under-20 World Cup.
He captained the French under-18 team.
He scored in the semi-final
of the 1996 UEFA under-18 championship.

In 1997 he won his first full cap
for France, against South Africa.

The next year Thierry was in the squad
for the World Cup finals in France.
He was only 20.
He scored against South Africa.
He scored twice against Saudi Arabia.
He scored a penalty against Italy.
France beat Brazil in the final 3–0.
France had won the World Cup.
And Thierry Henry was
France's top scorer.

Thierry and the France team after winning the 1998 World Cup.

After the World Cup Thierry went back
to the estate in Paris where he grew up.
Two thousand people came out to see him.

By Euro 2000 the French squad was full of
Arsenal players and ex-players.

Thierry scored against Denmark.
He scored against the Czech Republic.
He scored against Portugal.
France beat Italy 2–1 in the final.
Thierry was France's top scorer again.
He was voted man of the match three times.

Everyone thought France would win
the World Cup in 2002.
But Thierry just couldn't score.
France didn't score any goals.
They were knocked out.

Thierry scored six goals in seven qualifying
games for Euro 2004.
He scored twice against Switzerland
in the group stage.
But France were knocked out
by Greece in the quarter-finals.

So far Thierry has scored
27 goals in 66 games for his country.

4 Arsenal

In 1999 Italian giants Juventus
bought Thierry for £10 million.
He was only 22.
But Italian football was too defensive.
Juventus wanted him to play as a wing-back.
Thierry was not happy.
He only scored three goals.
He wanted to score more goals.

After six months he was sold again.
This time to Arsène Wenger and Arsenal,
the London club he supported as a boy.

Thierry Henry moved to Arsenal in August 1999.

Arsène Wenger wanted Thierry
to replace his old friend Nicholas Anelka.
Anelka was moving to Real Madrid.

There were other French players at Arsenal:
Petit, Vieira and Grimandi.

Wenger turned Thierry into a central striker.
It was hard at first.
Thierry took a while to adjust
to the Premier League.
He scored only two goals in his first 17 games.

But soon the goals started coming.
By the end of his first season
Thierry had scored 27 goals.

Defenders didn't know how to stop him.
He was so fast.
He was so clever.
One manager said the only way
to stop Thierry was to shoot him!

Thierry scoring for Arsenal in 2004.

The next season Thierry helped Arsenal
reach the quarter-finals of the Champions' League.
They were also runners-up in the Premier League
and in the FA Cup.

Since then, Thierry's goals have helped Arsenal
win the FA Cup twice,
and the Premier League twice.

Once he scored four goals against Leeds.
The next week he scored three goals
against Liverpool.
That's seven goals in two games!

You don't have to be an Arsenal fan
to like watching Thierry Henry.
Thanks to Thierry's goals, away fans can't sing
'boring, boring Arsenal' any more.

The Gunners love him.
They call him 'King Henry',
the king of Highbury's North Bank.

In 2003–4 Arsenal went all season
without losing a Premier League game.
No team had done this for 115 years.
Over three seasons they went 49 league games
without losing.
This is a record.

In his first five seasons at Highbury
Thierry scored 151 goals in 256 games.
He was the second fastest player ever
to score 100 goals in the Premier League.

He holds the Arsenal record for
scoring in ten games on the trot
in the Premiership.

Thierry is now the third highest scorer
in Arsenal's history.
Only Arsenal legends Ian Wright
and Cliff Bastin have
hit the back of the net more times.

It won't be long until Thierry beats
Ian Wright's record of 185 goals.

5 Superman

'When you put on the shirt of France or Arsenal,
you change,' says Thierry.
'It's like a new skin. You become Superman.'

Thierry is 188 cm (6 feet 2 inches) tall.
This is tall for such a fast player.
He turns quickly.
When he drops his left shoulder
he leaves defenders behind.
With his long legs he skips past them.

He doesn't score many goals with his head.
'The head is for thinking,' he says.

He scores a lot of goals,
but he isn't selfish.
He creates a lot of goals for his team-mates.
'It is important to score goals,' he says,
'but I don't see that as the main part of my game.
I like to run around and set people up for goals.'

Arsène Wenger says he is 'the best in the world'.
Jose Antonio Reyes calls him a 'galactico'.
This means he comes from another planet!
Arsenal chief David Dein says Thierry is
'the best player to ever pull on an Arsenal shirt'.

Chelsea tried to buy him but Arsenal said,
'Henry is not for sale at any price'.

Patrick Vieira calls his friend
'the best striker in the world'.
Vieira should know.
He has played against all the greats.

Thierry after Arsenal won the FA Cup in 2004.

6 Europe

In Thierry's first season with Arsenal during
1999–2000, he scored eight goals in the UEFA Cup.
Arsenal were in the final
but they lost against Galatasaray.

The next season when Arsenal were in
the Champions' League,
Thierry scored four goals.
He scored against Valencia in the quarter-finals.
But Valencia won on away goals.

Thierry scored 14 goals in the Champions' League
over the next two seasons.
He scored a hat-trick against AS Roma.
But it wasn't enough.
Each time Arsenal were knocked out
in the group stage of the competition.

In 2003–4 Arsenal reached the Champions' League
quarter-finals.
Thierry scored five goals.
He led Arsenal to a 5–1 win
over Inter Milan in Italy.
First he scored with a side-footed shot.
Then he crossed for Freddie Ljungberg
to score Arsenal's second goal.
With ten minutes to go
Thierry broke away with the ball.
He ran towards the goal.
He beat Zanetti and slid the ball
past Toldo and into the net.
The next day one Italian newspaper said,
'Kneel Down before the King'!
Everyone thought Arsenal
were going to win the cup this time.
But they were knocked out
by Chelsea in the quarter-final.

In his first five seasons at Arsenal
Thierry scored 31 goals in 69 European games.
This is another Arsenal record.

7 Va Va Voom

Thierry Henry earns £8 million a year.
His wife Claire is a model.
She played his girlfriend
in the Renault Clio adverts.
They were married at Highclere Castle
in Berkshire.
They live in a six-bedroom house in London
worth £9 million.

Thierry advertises Nike boots and Renault cars.
His friends call him Tel, Titi or Terry.
His favourite films are *The Usual Suspects*
and *Antwone Fisher*.

Thierry likes watching all sports on TV –
except darts and cricket!
And he doesn't like playing golf.

Thierry with his wife, Claire.

Thierry helps raise money for AIDS charities.
He gives money to a school
for footballers in Africa.
He has appeared in a film about
asylum-seekers and refugees.
When he won the Golden Boot
he gave the prize money to the Childline charity.

Thierry also supports Show Racism the Red Card.
As a black player he knows how stupid racists are.
But he never fights back –
except by using his football skills.
'The only answer I can give is on the pitch,'
he says.
And he does.

Thierry Henry is cool.
He is talented.
He has style.
He smiles a lot.
He is the best striker in the world.

Thierry Henry has lots of 'va va voom'. . .

Thierry raising money for the charity, Childline.

8 Honours and Stats

Club	Season	Goals	Games
Monaco	1994–1995	3	8
Monaco	1995–1996	3	23
Monaco	1996–1997	9	36
Monaco	1997–1998	4	30
Monaco	1998–1999	1	13
Juventus	1998–1999	2	16
Arsenal	1999–2000	27	47
Arsenal	2000–2001	22	44
Arsenal	2001–2002	35	55
Arsenal	2002–2003	35	57
Arsenal	2003–2004	41	50

1996	French Young Footballer of the Year
1997	Helped Monaco win the French League
1998	Helped France win the World Cup
2000	Helped France win the European Championship
2001	Awarded the Golden Boot Award
2002	Helped Arsenal win the FA Cup and the Premier League (the Double)
2003	Helped Arsenal win the FA Cup

2003	Voted French Personality of the Year
	Voted Premier League Player of the Year
2004	Voted Premier League Player of the Year
	Helped Arsenal win the Premier League
	Awarded the Golden Boot Award
	Voted runner-up European Player of of the Year
	Voted runner-up World Player of the Year